T0400920

Organize an
OCEAN

By William Anthony

BEARPORT
PUBLISHING

Minneapolis, Minnesota

Credits

All images are courtesy of Shutterstock.com unless otherwise specified. With thanks to Getty Images, Thinkstock Photo, and iStockphoto.

Cover – Maquiladora, CK Ma, Wonderful Nature, AurelioaPhoto, MicroOne, mallinka. 4–5 – Luma creative, Borisoff. 6–7 – Allexxandar, Filip Fuxa, Rvector, VectorPot. 8–9 – silvae, Richard Whitcombe, tn-prints, Alexander Ryabintsev. 10–11 – divedog, Wirestock Creators, LynxVector, Rvector, Andrew Krasovitckii, Derariad. 12–13 – Rich Carey, David A Litman, Eno Boy, Double Brain, LynxVector, KittyVector. 14–15 – Neil Bromhall, pongtap41, NPaveIN, AnnstasAg, udaix, Made by Marko. 16–17 – Luiz Felipe V. Puntel, AshtonEa, Oleg7799, Hennadii H, diluck, lukpedclub, trgrowth. 18–19 – California Academy of Sciences, CCO, via Wikimedia Commons, Eno Boy. 20–21 – OlegRi, noraismail, MuchMania, greenpic.studio, ByEmo. 22–23 – 123Done, AllNikArt, Leria Khmarka.

Library of Congress Cataloging-in-Publication Data is available at www.loc.gov or upon request from the publisher.

ISBN: 978-1-63691-483-1 (hardcover)
ISBN: 978-1-63691-488-6 (paperback)
ISBN: 978-1-63691-493-0 (ebook)

For more information, write to Bearport Publishing, 5357 Penn Avenue South, Minneapolis, MN 55419. Printed in the United States of America.

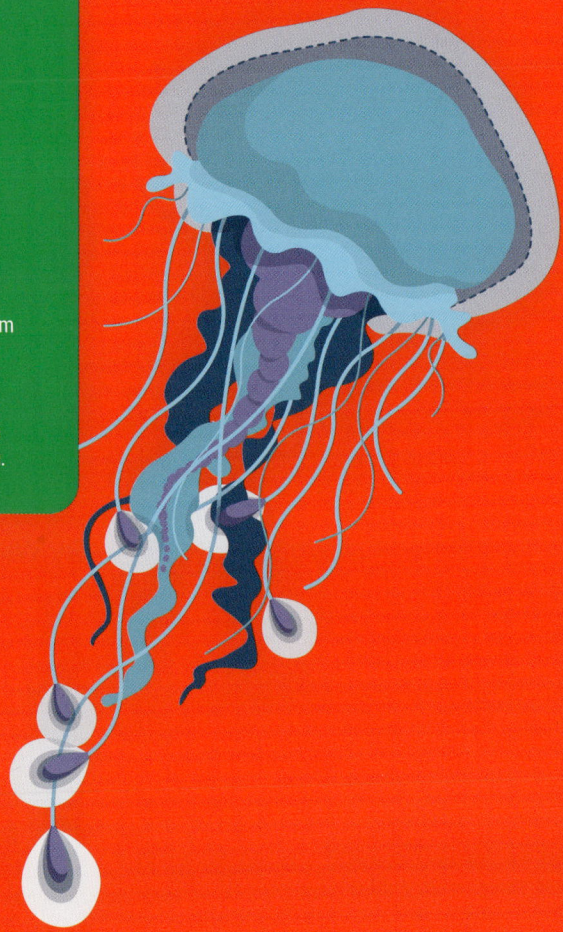

Contents

How to Build Our World

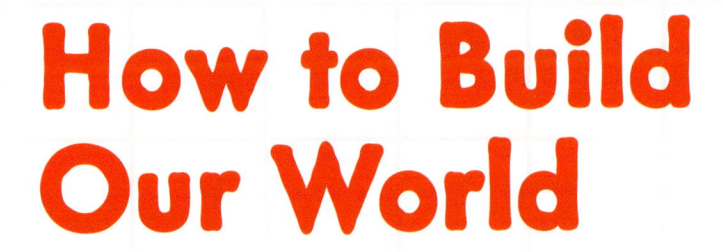

Our world is amazing. It is full of places to go and things to see. There are different **environments**, from oceans to rain forests. Each one has plants, animals, and more.

What does an ocean environment look like? Let's build one to find out!

Begin with Water

The first thing we need is water to fill our ocean! An ocean is a huge **body** of water.

Ocean water is salty. It is different from the water we drink.

Most of our planet is covered with ocean.

The ocean is very deep. It is split into different **layers** of water at different **depths**.

Let In the Life

Now that we've got the salt water, let's add some life to our ocean! The ocean is home to many different animals, plants, and other living things.

Coral and algae are two things that grow in the ocean.

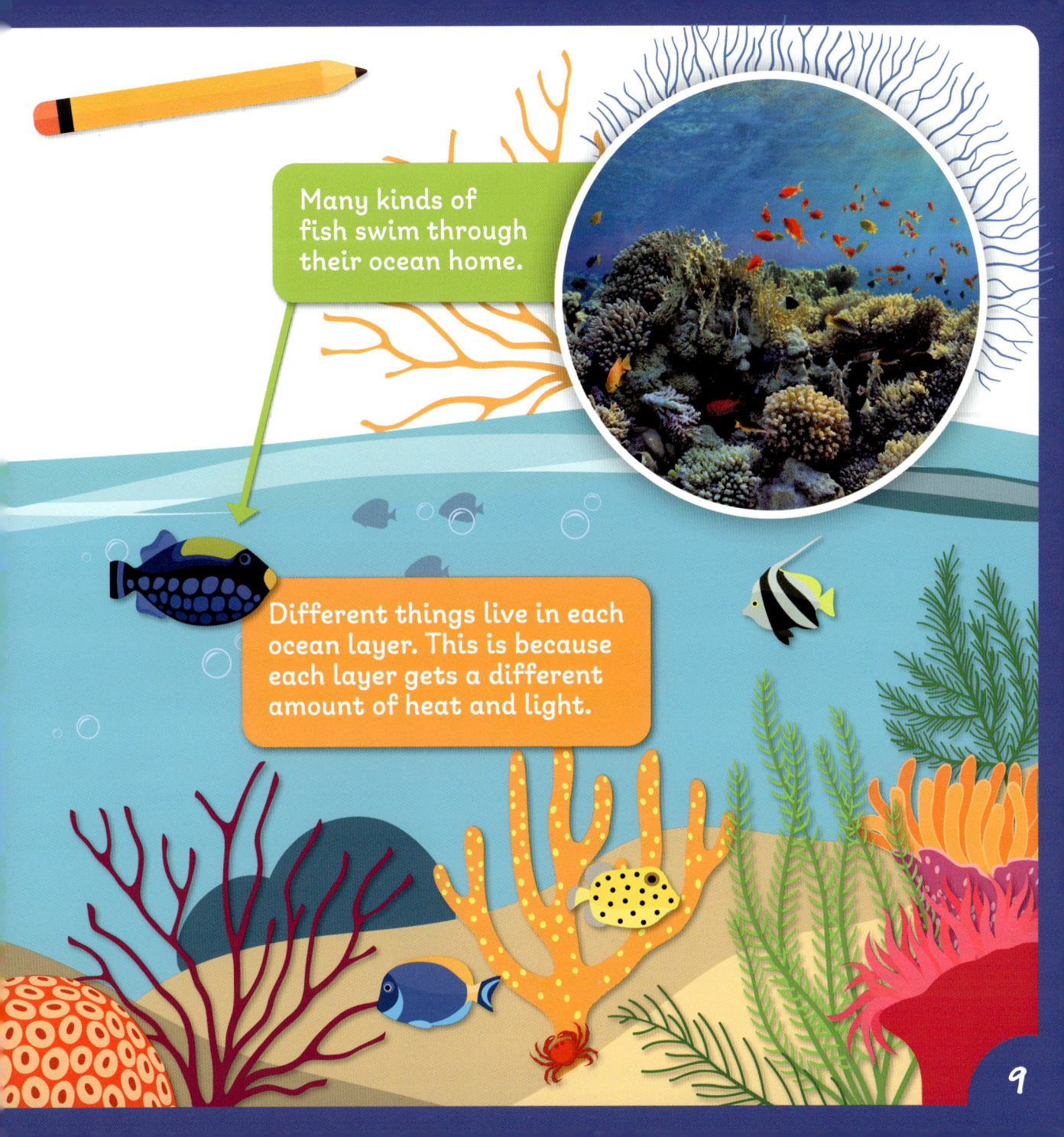

Many kinds of fish swim through their ocean home.

Different things live in each ocean layer. This is because each layer gets a different amount of heat and light.

Start Up the Sunlight Zone

Let's dive into the layers of our ocean, starting at the **surface**. The top layer is called the sunlight zone. It is the closest layer to the sun, so it gets the most sunlight!

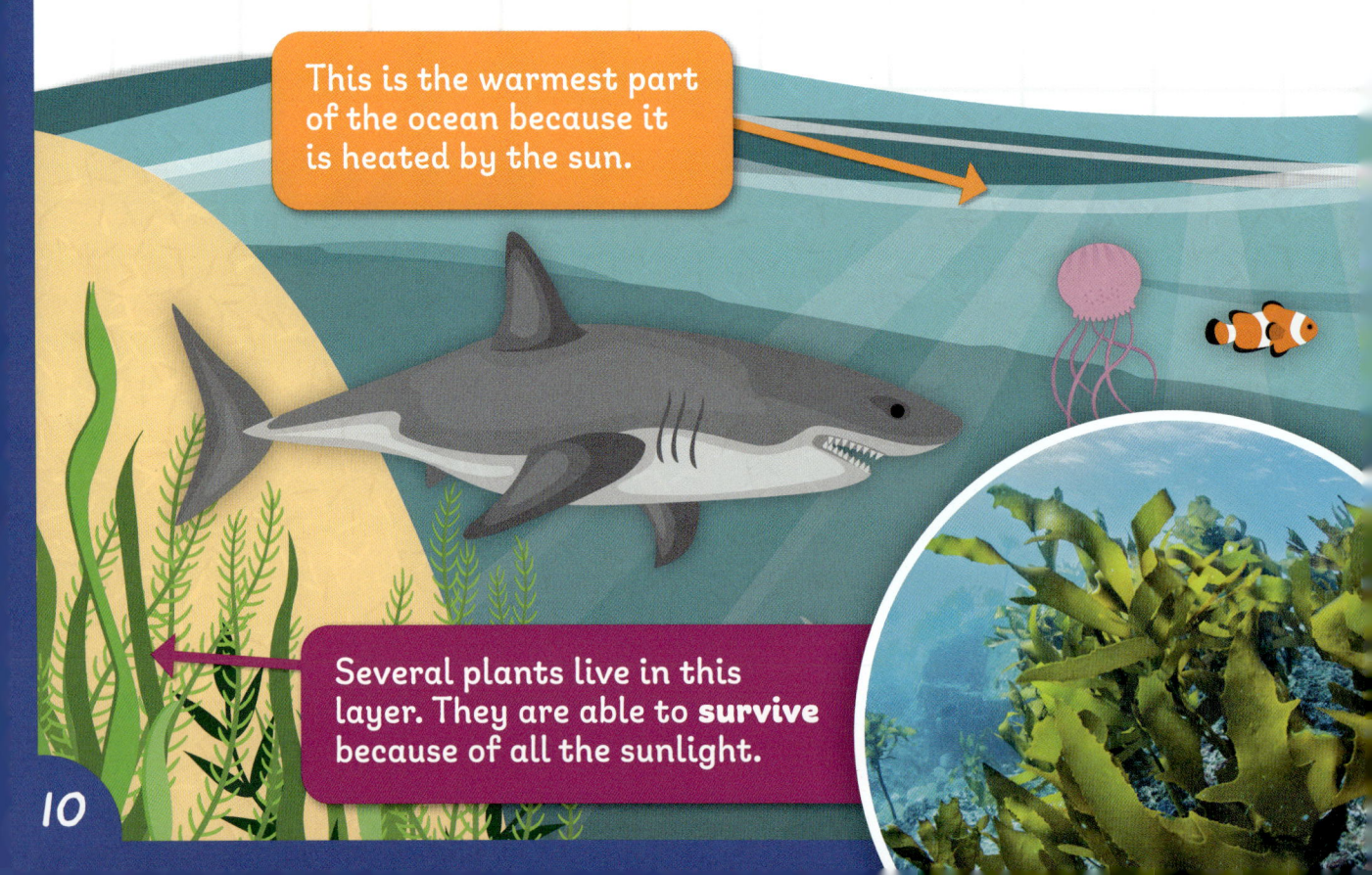

This is the warmest part of the ocean because it is heated by the sun.

Several plants live in this layer. They are able to **survive** because of all the sunlight.

Lots of animals live in the sunlight zone, including sharks, seals, and crabs.

Create the Twilight Zone

As we dive down deeper, we'll build our ocean's next layer. It is called the twilight zone.

The twilight zone gets less light than the sunlight zone. This means fewer plants can live in this layer.

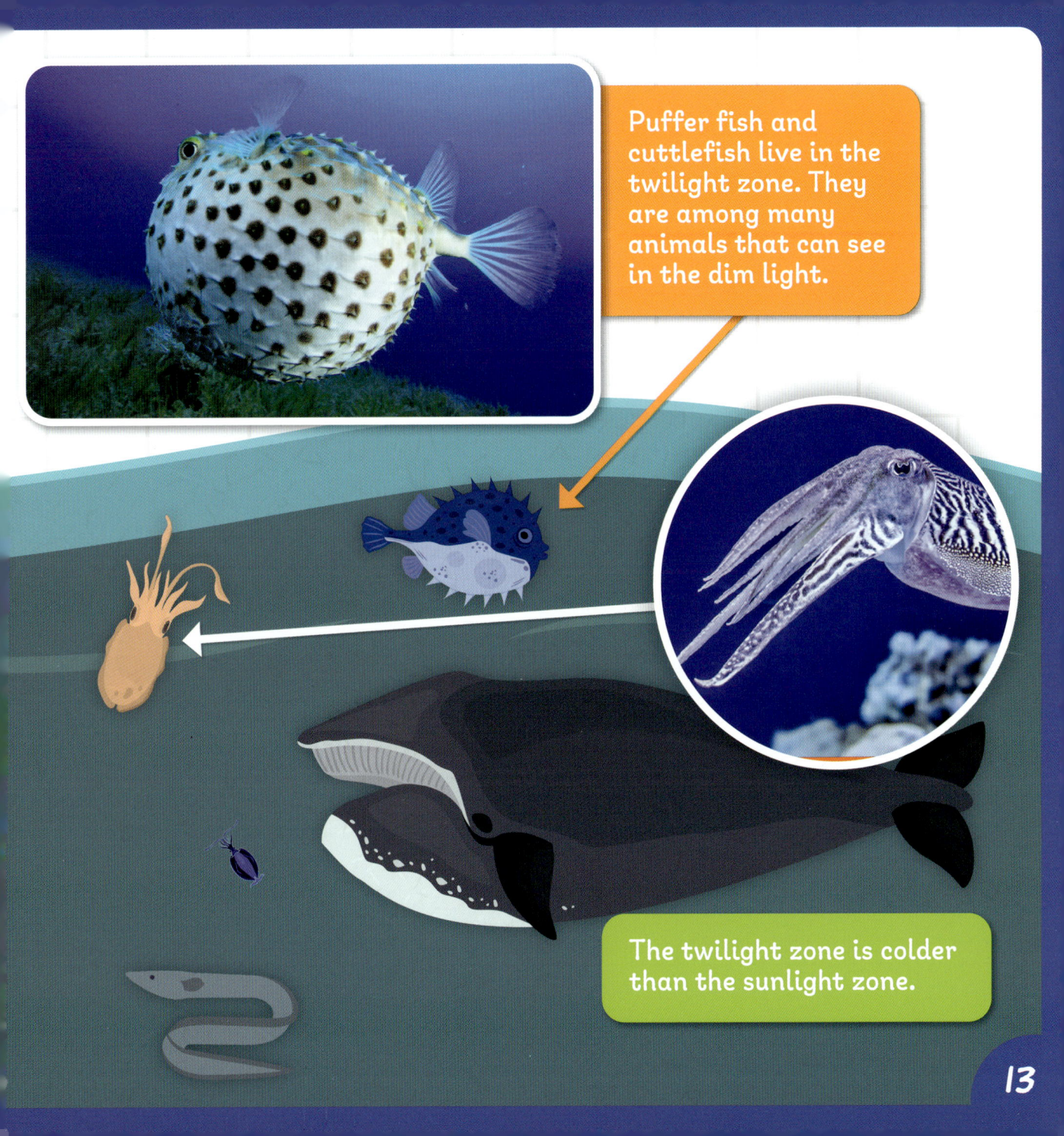

Puffer fish and cuttlefish live in the twilight zone. They are among many animals that can see in the dim light.

The twilight zone is colder than the sunlight zone.

13

Make the Midnight Zone

Who turned out the lights? Deeper into our ocean is a dark layer called the midnight zone.

There is no sunlight this deep in the ocean. It is very cold.

Plants cannot survive in the midnight zone.

The only light in this layer is made by animals themselves.

Arrange the Abyss

Below the midnight zone is the abyss. In some places, this is the deepest layer of the ocean. It is very cold and completely dark!

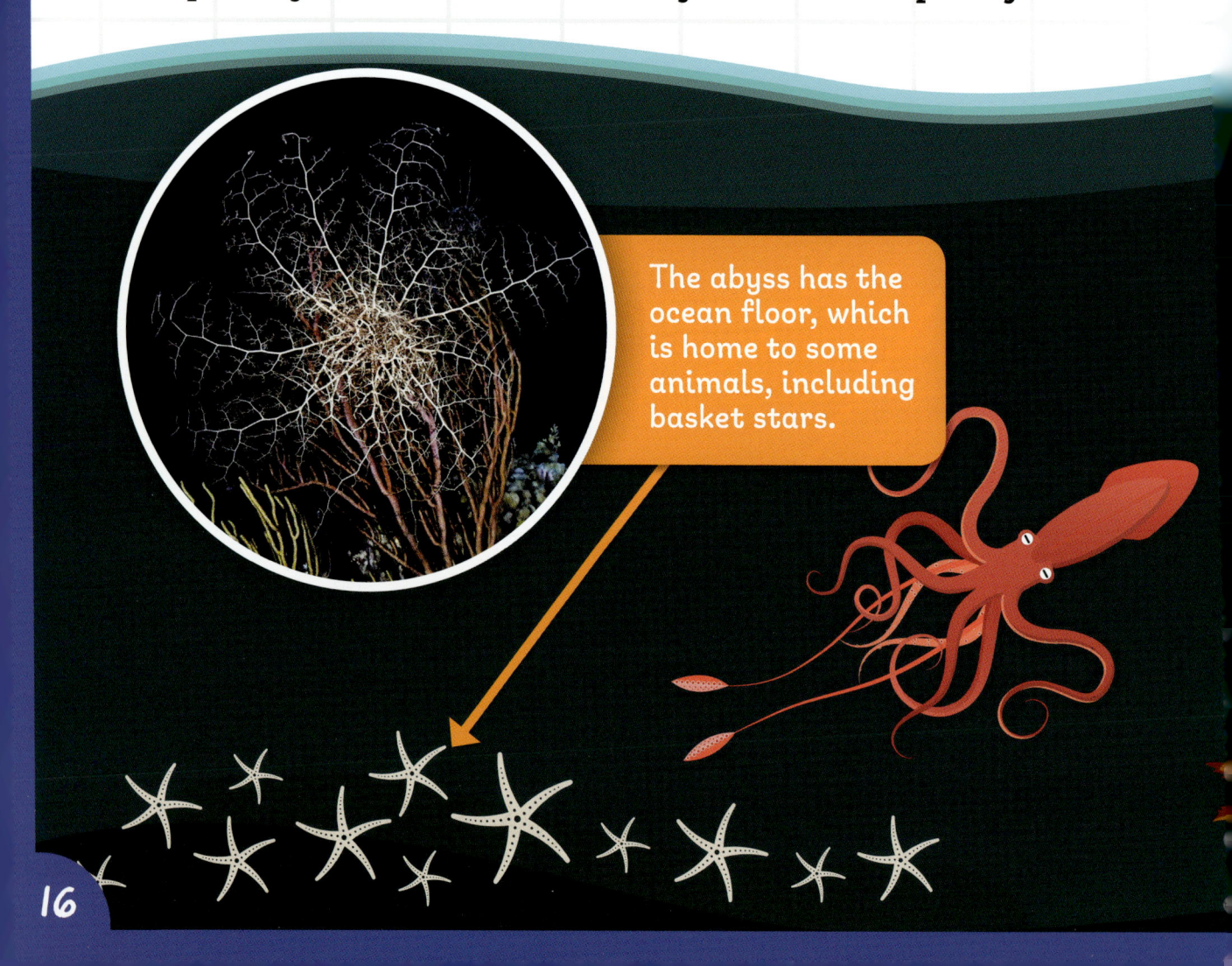

The abyss has the ocean floor, which is home to some animals, including basket stars.

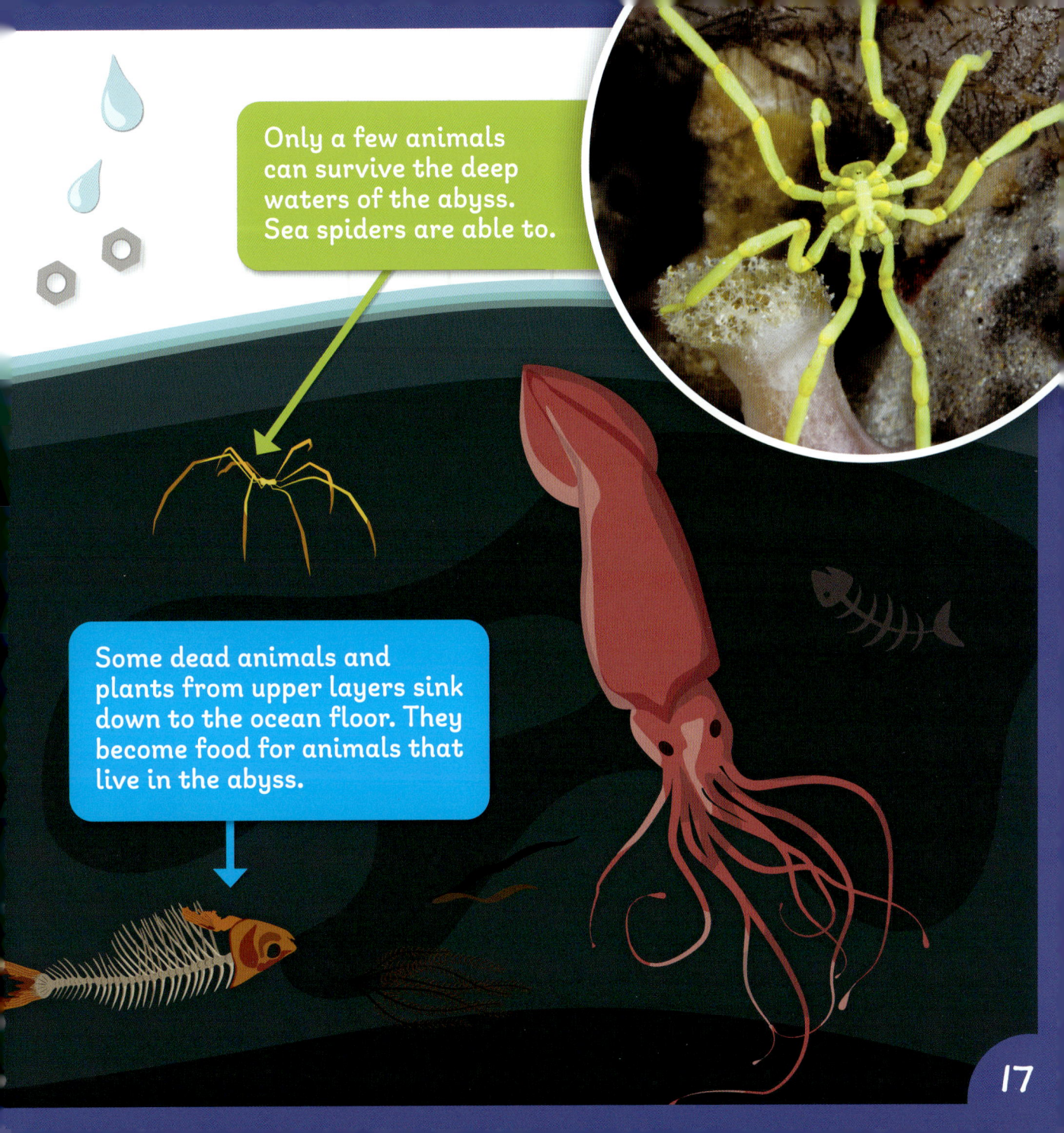

Only a few animals can survive the deep waters of the abyss. Sea spiders are able to.

Some dead animals and plants from upper layers sink down to the ocean floor. They become food for animals that live in the abyss.

Add the Trenches

There are some places where we can go even deeper than the abyss. Let's dig some trenches into our ocean floor!

Only some parts of the ocean floor have long, deep holes called trenches. They are some of the deepest places on Earth.

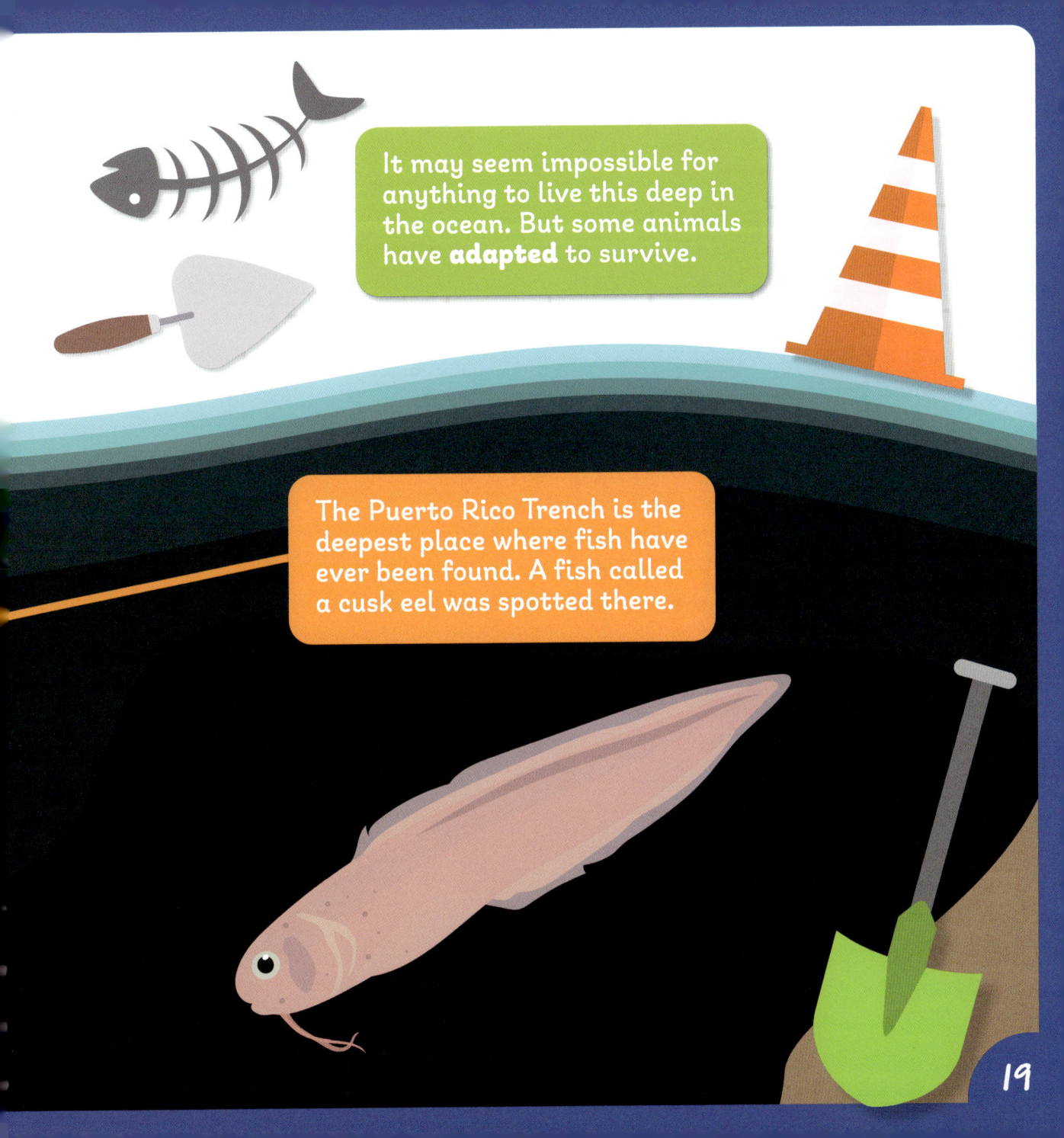

It may seem impossible for anything to live this deep in the ocean. But some animals have **adapted** to survive.

The Puerto Rico Trench is the deepest place where fish have ever been found. A fish called a cusk eel was spotted there.

Explore the Ocean

Now that we've built all the layers of our ocean, let's find ways to explore it!

Submarines help us dive down to the deep parts of the ocean.

We can use different **vehicles** to travel around the ocean.

Boats let us explore the surface of the ocean.

Make Your Own Environment

Ocean environments are incredible! They are full of fantastic living things. Now, it's time to build your own environment! You could draw it, paint it, or write about it. What do you want to put in your ocean?

Will your ocean end with the abyss, or will you include trenches?

Which animals will live in your ocean?

Which vehicles will you use to explore your ocean?

Glossary

adapted changed over time to fit the environment

algae tiny plantlike living things that grow in water

body a whole area of something

coral rocklike structures made from the skeletons of sea animals also called coral

depths areas that are far below the surface

environments the different parts of our world in which people, animals, and plants live

layers parts of something that are set one on top of another

surface the top part of something

survive to stay alive

vehicles machines used to carry people or things from one place to another

Index